Ren Women of Cornwall

Carolyn Martin

Bossiney Books • Exeter

The women in this book were not all Cornish by birth but include incomers who made an impact within the county. Several remarkable women appear in *Cornwall's Writers* in this series, so their biographies are not duplicated here.

The text has partly been drawn from *Cornwall's People*, published in 2009.

Cornwall's Writers

includes the following remarkable authors
Daphne du Maurier
Helen Dunmore
Kitty Lee Jenner
Rosamunde Pilcher
'Mary Wesley'
Anne Treneer

First published 2024 by
Bossiney Books Ltd, 68 Thorndale Courts, Whitycombe Way, Exeter, EX4 2NY
www.bossineybooks.com
ISBN 978-1-915664-24-2

Acknowledgements
Cover artwork by Beth Paisley

Printed in Great Britain by Deltor, Saltash, Cornwall

Thomasine Blight ('Tammy Blee')   1793-1856
Wise woman or witch

Tammy Blee, the famous 'wise woman' or, as some would say, witch, was born Thomasine Williams in Gwennap in 1793. She married Richard Blight at Redruth in 1825 and they had at least three children, though one died shortly after birth, and Richard himself died in 1832.

In 1835 she remarried. Her second husband James Thomas, 'engine man', was ten years younger than her, which may suggest that she was a relatively wealthy widow or was prospering in her trade, and in 1841 they were living in Back Lane, Redruth.

Both Tammy and James spent an increasing part of their time as 'pellers', claiming to cure people, animals, and even on occasion mine machinery, of various ills. They also warded off future disasters which they said were imminent, and both probably made a good living from these activities.

The historical evidence inevitably comes from writers who were keen to emphasise their own scepticism and who tend to concentrate on the presumed greed of the pellers and the gullibility of their clients. No doubt then, as today, some such practitioners were rogues and mountebanks, whilst the majority were sincerely convinced that what they were doing was effective – and indeed perhaps it often was, since they had powerful herbal remedies at their disposal, as well as those two great healers, time and the placebo effect.

At least they probably did less damage than most nineteenth century doctors.

It is likely that Tammy was well-intentioned, but she may have regretted introducing her second husband to the profession. The *West Briton* of 27 Nov 1863 reported on a 'wise man' from Illogan, subsequently named as James Thomas,

> married some time since to the late celebrated Tammy Blee of Redruth, who afterwards removed to Helston and carried on as a fortune teller, but parted from her husband James Thomas on account of a warrant for his apprehension having been issued against him by the magistrates of St Ives, from attempting to take a spell from Mrs Paynter, through her husband William Paynter, who stated before the magistrates that he wanted to commit a disgraceful offence. Thomas absconded and was absent from the

west of Cornwall for upwards of two years. His wife then stated that the virtue was in her, not in him; that she was of the real 'Peller' blood; and that he could tell nothing but through her.

James Thomas's main clients seem to have been young sailors from Hayle, whose ships could be kept safe from witchcraft if they slept with him and paid for the privilege, but he also toured the Roseland every few months in a horse and cart, selling protection against impending doom.

After leaving James Thomas, Tammy moved to Helston, where she changed her official name back to Thomasine Blight and shared her house with her son William and a young cousin. There her personal fame continued to grow, so much so that people even came on foot from St Buryan to consult her. She died on 6 October 1856.

James Thomas continued his dubious career, but with greater discretion, till his death in February 1874.

Thomasin Bonaventure c1440-1512
Merchant and philanthropist

Thomasine Bonaventure was a great benefactor to Week St Mary, and a legendary version of her story is part of Cornish folklore.

This version suggests that she was a poor girl who was tending sheep in the fields when a rich London merchant passed by, spotted her, took a liking to her, and persuaded her parents to let her go to London with him, to be a servant to his wife. The wife died, the merchant married Thomasine, then promptly died himself. As a wealthy widow she was snapped up by another merchant, he died, and the even wealthier widow was snapped up by the Lord Mayor of London. Then he died and she devoted all her wealth to charity in her native parish.

It is hard not to raise an eyebrow, especially since Bonaventure is hardly a common Cornish surname but *buona ventura* is Italian for good luck, so she is 'Tamsin Success-Story'. Surely this cannot have been her real name?

The legend is part true, part false. Her parents really were John and Joan Bonaventure of Week St Mary, but they were gentry. She went to London into the household of a family friend, to learn the art of housekeeping as was the norm at that time, and there married Henry Galle, a wealthy tailor. He died in 1466. She inherited the business, ran it herself for a time then formed a simultaneous business and marital merger with Thomas Barnaby – who died within the year.

In 1469 she married again. Her third husband, Thomas Percyvale (1430-1503), was a leading merchant who was knighted in 1485 and served as Lord Mayor in 1498. He endowed a free grammar school in his native Macclesfield, which later became the King's School.

Thomasine continued to manage the business and was famously rich – sufficiently so to be obliged to hand the king a 'loan' of £1000. Like her husband, she believed in education and she endowed a free school (the first in Cornwall) at Week St Mary, as well as a chantry, and gave money for road and bridge repair and many other charitable causes within the parish. She died in 1512 and was buried in London.

The folklore Thomasine could have been a flirt who struck lucky. The real Thomasine was much more interesting – a shrewd business-woman who made her own fortune, and then chose to spend it on charitable projects in the village of her birth.

Mary Bryant (née Broad) 1765-1845
Petty thief, convict and epic survivor

Mary Bryant was born in Fowey, to William Broad, a sailor, and his wife Grace (née Symons). Times were hard for the family and when she was seventeen, Mary travelled to Plymouth in search of work. Desperate for money, she took to petty thieving. In 1786, she was apprehended for stealing a silk bonnet from Agnes Lakeman on the public highway. Mary was sentenced to death at Exeter Lenten Assizes, a sentence that was later commuted to seven years transportation.

Prisoners waiting for a passage were housed in the *Dunkirk*, an old warship moored off Plymouth. Here Mary met William Bryant, a fisherman from Fowey, who was later to become her husband, and Watkin Tench, who was to reappear in her life subsequently. Mary's daughter Charlotte was born during the voyage to Sydney. Conditions on the ship were unsanitary, crowded and often violent, with many deaths. Mary was a survivor and soon after arrival in Australia she married William Bryant; their son Emanuel was born in 1790. (Charlotte was not William Bryant's child.)

Given certain privileges as a married couple, Mary and William Bryant exploited their knowledge of the sea by taking responsibility for fishing in Sydney Harbour. William was apprehended for profiting privately from the sale of the catch and the lashes he received as punishment hardened his determination to escape. With maps and other navigational aids obtained from the captain of a passing Dutch trading vessel – in return for favours from Mary – the couple, the two children and seven other convicts slipped away in the Governor's boat.

Despite storms and hunger, landing wherever they could for food and water, the crew finally reached Koepay in Timor, after three long months at sea. Here they claimed to be shipwreck survivors and were clothed and fed while waiting for a passage back to Britain. Unfortunately William Bryant, probably drunk, admitted that they had escaped from the penal colony, so they were all detained and put on board a ship to Batavia (now Jakarta). Here, both William Bryant and Emanuel died. The remaining four convicts, Mary and Charlotte, were eventually shipped back to England from Cape Town, on board the *Gorgon*, whose captain, Watkin Tench, showed particular kindness. Sadly, Charlotte died during the journey and was buried at sea.

On arrival in England in 1792, Mary was imprisoned in Newgate and she expected to be sent back to Australia. By chance, her story was taken up by the national newspapers and came to the notice of James Boswell, the biographer of Dr Johnson. He pressed the Home Secretary for a pardon and this was granted in May 1793. Demonstrating true compassion, Boswell gave Mary an annuity of £10 and at the request of her family Mary returned to Fowey. To show her gratitude, she presented Boswell with a packet of dried Australian 'sweet tea' leaves, carried all the way from Sydney Cove. Mary is said to have spent about three years in Fowey before moving away, possibly to Breage, although there are no further reliable records of her life, or death.

Rowena Cade 1893-1983
Founder of the Minack Theatre

Dorothy Mary Rowena Cade was born at Spondon on the edge of Derby, where the family had deep roots. Her father Charles Cade managed a cotton mill and the painter Joseph Wright of Derby was her great-great-grandfather. Her mother was Mary Rowena Smelt, a Wiltshire clergyman's daughter.

Rowena took part in amateur theatricals as a child. In 1906 when her father retired, the family moved to genteel Cheltenham.

During WW1, Rowena selected and broke horses to be shipped out to the front line. After the war, and her father's death, Rowena and her mother moved several times before renting a house at Lamorna. Rowena then bought the Minack headland for £100, and built a house there using local stone.

In 1929 Rowena was wardrobe mistress for an amateur outdoor production of *A Midsummer Night's Dream*, then in 1931, looking for a suitable outdoor venue for *The Tempest*, she had an inspiration to use the Minack site. It took massive efforts to build a stage and seating of sorts in this exposed gully, and at least one wheelbarrow was lost over the cliff. Whilst much of the manual work was done by Billy Rawlings and Charles Thomas Angove, her gardeners, Rowena herself carried sand for concrete, and even large timbers, up from the beach on her back. She continued with the physical work until in her mid-eighties.

The theatre was improved greatly after the production of *The Tempest*, then came the war. Much damage was done as a result of coastal defence structures; substantial repairs were needed after 1945.

During the war, Rowena Cade was the local billeting officer for evacuees.

Because the summer drama season was always short, the theatre never paid its way, and was supported from Rowena's own pocket. In 1976, she presented the theatre and nearby land to a charitable trust, which has been able to carry her work forward. She died in 1983.

Elizabeth Catherine Thomas Carne 1817-1873
Geologist and philanthropist

Elizabeth Carne's father was a well known geologist and his daughter followed in his footsteps. She was born in Phillack in west Cornwall, the fifth of the six children of Mary Thomas and Joseph Carne, director of the Cornish Copper Company. As well as a respected geologist, he was also a strong Methodist and the local Methodist bookroom was housed at their home.

Elizabeth Carne was educated at home, together with her sisters, while the family were living in Chapel Street, Penzance. She read widely, studied mathematics and was well versed in languages. She also helped her father to arrange his large mineral collection. None of her sisters shared this interest and when he died in 1858 he left his collection and cases to Elizabeth, 'because she knows more and is more attached to the science of mineralogy than my other daughters'. This was as well as the sum of £22,000 and the house in Chapel Street. She also took over the family bank, Batten, Carne & Carne, on her father's death.

Aware of the poverty around her, like her father she donated money to local causes. She gave the site for St Paul's school in Penzance and founded schools at Wesley Rock (Heamoor), Carfury and Bosullow. In addition, in 1861 she gave £200 for the land on which St John's Hall and the new museum for the Royal Geological Society of Cornwall was to be built. Her later offer to build a new wing for her father's collection of minerals as well as finance new galleries and heating for the museum was rejected. The collection later went to the Sedgwick Museum in the University of Cambridge.

Elizabeth Carne was the first woman to be elected as a member of the Society in 1865, a rare honour.

Her interest in geology was unusual for a woman at that time. Not only did she introduce original ideas but she wrote learned scientific papers and presented these to the Royal Geological Society of Cornwall. Four papers were written in total, with several books and work for the *London Quarterly Review*. She was particularly interested in the formation of granite, an interest shared with her father.

She made two trips abroad, to Pau for a rest and to Menton where she studied the geology of the French Alps. Her later years were spent organizing her father's collection, together with her sister. She died in Penzance in 1873 and was buried at Phillack.

Mary Coate 1886-1972
Historian

Mary Coate was the author of *Cornwall in the Great Civil War and Interregnum 1642-1660*, an authoritative and scholarly account of the events of the time.

She was a member of a large family brought up in rural Dorset, followed by some years in Middlesex, then a country parsonage in Bedfordshire. Her father, Harry Coate, was Canon of Lidlington and her mother, Henrietta, came from Melbourne, Australia. Educated at Bedford High School, Coate taught for a few years before entering St Hilda's Hall, Oxford, in 1912. She was awarded a first class honours degree in Modern History in 1915 and moved to Cornwall as a lecturer at the Diocesan Training College, Truro.

In 1922, she took up a position as History Tutor at Lady Margaret

Hall, Oxford – women had been admitted as full members of the university in 1920 – where she remained until her retirement in 1946. Always interested in the welfare of her students, she encouraged them to maximise their potential and at the same time she undertook her own research on a wide variety of topics. She published *Cornwall in the Great Civil War* in 1933 and *The Vyvyan Family of Trelowarren* in 1950.

Coate had been granted a Travelling Fellowship to study the Conde de Gondomar, Spanish ambassador to the court of James I, but with the outbreak of WW2 she was unable to take up the award and travel to Spain.

After retirement, with the death of the Professor of History at Exeter University, she stepped in to organise the work of the department until a successor could be found. Living in Devon, she was Chairman of the Devon and Cornwall Record Society and a member of the Devon and Cornwall Committee of the National Register of Archives. She was made Emeritus Fellow of Lady Margaret Hall in 1954.

Margaret Ann Courtney 1834-1929
Folklorist

Writing about customs and legends in West Penwith, Margaret Ann Courtney did much to enhance our knowledge of Cornish folklore. She was born and spent most of her life in Penzance, the eldest daughter of John Sampson Courtney, a banker's clerk then cashier, and his wife Sarah (née Mortimer), who came from the Isles of Scilly. Her father had been born in Ilfracombe and when he moved to Penzance in 1823 he wrote a detailed account of the town. His daughter, Margaret Ann must have inherited his interest in local history. Between 1880 and 1890, she published books on Cornish folklore, including *Cornish Feasts and 'Feasten' Customs, Folklore and Legends of Cornwall* and *A Glossary of Words in use in West Cornwall*.

The books have been reprinted over the years and were written in an engaging and informal style, leading the reader from one anecdote to another. She recounts, for example, that Good Friday was more a feast than a fast and that the custom was still retained along the Helford River, where shellfish were – and still are – collected and eaten on the day.

The family fortunes improved greatly when her father was promoted to acting manager at Bolitho's Bank in Penzance in 1856 and they moved from New Street to a more prestigious address at Alverton House. After the death of her mother in 1859, Margaret Courtney looked after her father and younger siblings. Her older brother Leonard Henry was a politician of some note, as MP for Liskeard and then for Bodmin, Financial Secretary to the Treasury and Deputy Speaker.

Elizabeth Adela Forbes (née Armstrong) 1859-1912
Artist

Elizabeth Forbes was born in Ontario, daughter of William Robertson Armstrong and Frances (née Hawksley). She received instruction at home before travelling to London with her mother at the age of 14 to attend the South Kensington Art Schools. She said later that she had been too young to appreciate the tuition fully. Staying with her uncle in Cheyne Walk, Chelsea, she lived next door to the painter Dante Gabriel Rossetti and, through her reading, she became drawn towards the Pre-Raphaelite movement. This is shown to advantage in her later imaginative illustrated books, of which *King Arthur's Wood* is the best known, published in 1904 and dedicated to her only child Alec (born 1893).

Further studies took Forbes to New York, Munich, Brittany, Holland and finally to Newlyn in 1885. It was here that she met Stanhope Forbes; they married in 1889, setting up their own art school in 1899.

Elizabeth Adela Forbes was a gifted artist, working in a wide variety of media, but following her marriage she lived in the shadow of her husband. She exhibited widely and her skill in drypoint etchings was admired by both Whistler and Sickert, although she did not pursue her etching in Cornwall.

She was admitted to the Royal Society of Painter-Etchers and Engravers and to the Royal Watercolour Society. Her paintings received much critical acclaim and she was awarded several medals. Her portrayal of children was particularly sympathetic, as in 'School is Out' (exhibited at the Royal Academy in 1889). One of the few female artists within the community, her obituary referred to her as the 'Queen of Newlyn' when she died at the age of 53.

Caroline Fox 1819-1871
Diarist

A member of the well-known Quaker family in Falmouth, Caroline Fox is remembered as a diarist. She was born at the family home at

Penjerrick and was the second daughter of Robert Were Fox and his wife Maria (née Barclay). She received an enlightened education at home with private tutors, including tuition in science and languages.

Later she made extended visits to the continent, and her meetings with scientists, writers and politicians are recorded in her diaries.

Together with other members of the Fox family, Caroline Fox helped to establish the Cornwall Polytechnic Society in Falmouth in 1833 (it became 'Royal' from 1835), an organisation designed to 'stimulate the ingenuity of the young, to promote industrious habits among the working classes and to elicit the inventive powers of the community at large'.

This concern for others was also reflected in her prison visits in London with Elizabeth Fry, as well as in her support for the Anti-Slavery Society. At meetings of the British Association for the Advancement of Science she met many of the eminent scientists of the day, some of whom were entertained at Penjerrick. The list of names included Michael Faraday, the philosopher John Stuart Mill, Thomas Carlyle, Tennyson and the artist Holman Hunt.

Fox was an engaging diarist and her perceptive, objective observations give an insight into both family life and the intellectual society of her time. Unfortunately, only a selection of her diaries survived. She instructed her sister, Anna Maria, to burn the diaries after her death, but a relative published an edited version in 1882, with other editions appearing in 1883 and more recently in 1972. By chance an early manuscript (1832-34) was discovered at Penjerrick and this has survived intact.

After 1860, Fox helped her sister to care for their brother Barclay Fox's four orphaned children. She held Bible classes with other Quakers in Falmouth and wrote a series of articles on religious themes. Bronchitis restricted her towards the end of her life and she was buried at the Quaker burial ground at Budock.

Ann Glanville 1796-1880

Champion rower

A champion rower who achieved national success, racing a four-oared waterman's boat with her all-women crew.

Ann Warren (Warring) was born in Saltash in 1796. She married

John Glanville and they had 14 children. Her husband worked as a waterman, ferrying passengers across the River Tamar but when he became unwell and could no longer work, Ann took over from him. This was unusual work for a woman at that time but Ann had a family to support and was an experienced rower.

Together with four other female rowers, Ann competed in local regattas and later in other gig-racing competitions. The ladies were distinctive with their white dresses and white caps and achieved considerable success, often beating all-male crews in different parts of the country. On one occasion, in Fleetwood, they were watched by Queen Victoria who congratulated Ann for her win against an all-male crew. However when they visited Le Havre in 1842, the French crew refused to compete against women. It was left to Ann to organize a demonstration competition between the female rowers and the crew of the paddle steamer *Grand Turk*. Naturally the race was won by the women.

In later years, Ann achieved local notoriety by rowing around the warships anchored in the Tamar, chatting with the crews. Then in 1879 when the Prince of Wales and the Duke of Edinburgh visited Plymouth, they invited Ann to lunch with them on their yacht. Tall and strong, she continued rowing well into her sixties.

In Saltash Ann is remembered with affection. A blue plaque marks the house where she lived between 1845 and 1880 and the Caradon Gig Rowing Club named their first pilot gig after her. In 2013, a fibre glass statue of Ann, sitting on a bench, was unveiled in Fore Street, Saltash, with an optional sound recording to listen to the achievements of her life. In 2018 the statue was moved to its current location, Saltash Waterside.

Ann died in 1880 and her funeral was well attended, all paid for by Admiral Lord Beresford. A Royal Marines band played the funeral march and she was buried in St Stephen-by-Saltash chuchyard.

Mary Grenfell 1841-1926
Miner's wife

At the beginning of the nineteenth century, the tin mines in Cornwall were flourishing and the young men in the Penwith area could always find work as miners. However by the end of the century, with the import of cheaper tin from abroad, particularly from Malaysia, coupled with the increasing cost of mining the deeper seams of tin, many mines closed or reduced their work force. As a consequence many skilled miners found themselves out of work, with no income to support themselves or families. Their expertise was sought abroad, in such countries as Mexico, South Africa or as far away as Australia. In order to seek their fortune, many miners left Cornwall and travelled overseas, leaving behind their wives and children. How the wives coped without the support of their husbands is an aspect of history that has long been forgotten. Mary Grenfell is one such example, although this time her husband went in search of gold.

Mary was born in 1841, the daughter of Mary Wall (née Bolitho) and William Ward, a miner. She was the eldest of their 14 children. At this time, the family were living in a miner's cottage in Carnyorth, Pendeen, which they owned. Mary must have received some basic education because she boasted that she could read and write at a young age. By the time she was 20, she was working as a tin ore dresser and contributing to the family income.

Mary married William Grenfell in 1862, another miner, and they lived at Trewellard in West Penwith. Their first two children died young but then they went on to have three more children, Mary, Martha and William.

With little work for experienced miners in Cornwall, William decided to seek work in Colorado. Not mining for tin this time, but gold. For the first four months, William sent money to Mary, but then the payments stopped. Back home in Cornwall, with no income, Mary found it difficult to care for her young family. In addition, she had to cope with the added tragedy of the death of her eldest daughter, Mary.

Eventually she found work as a live-in maid in Penzance. Her children were cared for by other family members in Carnyorth and the only time she saw them was on Sunday afternoons, her day off. She would leave her place of employment after lunch, walk to her mother's house for tea and to see her children, then walk back to Penzance before 10 pm. This was a round trip of some 15 miles.

In 1879 Mary decided to join her husband in Colorado. Her brother was already out there and probably paid for her journey. She travelled on the *Brittanic*, with William (5) and Martha (3) but on arrival in New York she was held up and when they eventually arrived in Denver, Mary was told that her husband had died of a fever and had been buried just a few days earlier. His fellow miners had tried to delay the funeral until her arrival, but had been unable to do so. Then within weeks, Martha caught measles and died. She was buried alongside her father in Bald Mountain cemetery.

The miners from St Just took pity on Mary and built her a rough wooden shelter. In return she set about cooking and laundering for 24 miners, working from four in the morning until midnight. With this income, she was able to open a boarding house for St Just miners, and one of the lodgers was her cousin, Andrew Stevens. They married in 1880 and Lillie Evelyn, their daughter, was born in 1882. Mary then returned to Cornwall with William and Lillie, together with her husband, sailing on the *Germanic*, from New York to Liverpool. Sadly, Andrew contracted tuberculosis and died in 1898.

The family gave Mary two somewhat dilapidated cottages in Carnyorth. She set about repairing these and made them into a single dwelling, Wesley House, (later renamed as Frimley House), living there with her daughter Lillie who was now married with a family. Despite the tribulations of her life, Mary lived to a good age, 84. She died in 1926.

Winifred (Fryniwyd) Margaret Jesse Harwood
(pseudonym F. Tennyson Jesse) 1888-1958
Author and criminologist

In her day, Tennyson Jesse was well known as a respected criminologist and author. What is not so well known is that she had artistic leanings and spent some time with the artistic community in Newlyn in West Cornwall. It was here that she took the name Fryniwyd (Fryn) although she wrote as F. Tennyson Jesse.

Tennyson Jesse was born in Chislehurst, Kent, the second daughter of the Reverend Eustace Tennyson d'Eyncourt Jesse, a high Anglican clergyman and Edith Louisa James who had Cornish family connections and was a great niece of the poet laureate Alfred Lord Tennyson. As her father did not have a settled position, the family travelled widely, at home and abroad. Tennyson Jesse remembered a series of lodgings as she attended different day schools.

She came to Cornwall in 1906, with her cousin, Cicely. The aim was to study at the Newlyn School of painting with Stanhope and Elizabeth Forbes. While there they lived at Myrtle Cottage, Newlyn, together with the painter Dod Shaw (later Dod Procter, see page 25). Tennyson Jesse

14

exhibited some of her pictures in Newlyn but then Elizabeth Forbes (see page 10) gave her the opportunity to act as editor of her publication *Paper Chase*. Having decided that she preferred writing to painting, she returned to London in 1911.

Her first position was working for *The Times* but she wrote short stories too. Her first short story, *The Mask*, was well reviewed, so much so that the playwright Harold Marsh Harwood (they married in 1918) wanted to produce it as a play. Then the publisher William Heinemann, offered to publish her first novel.

Around this time Tennyson Jesse suffered an unfortunate accident. While embarking on a trip on a pusher aircraft over Lake Windemere, as she waved to spectators she inadvertently caught her hand in the propeller. The result was the loss of two fingers and surgery on her hand. Later she went to New York where a mechanical device was fitted. The accident led to a dependence on morphine to ease the pain, as well as bouts of depression.

Undaunted, Tennyson Jesse set about travelling and writing; first of all to the Belgian front, acting as war correspondent for the *Daily Mail* – one of few women to do this work – then to France and Holland. The Ministry of Information asked her to write about the women's army, resulting in *The Sword of Deborah* in 1919.

During 1920s and the 1930s she continued writing and travelling, producing books on different subjects and taking an interest in the famous criminal trials of the day. Her knowledge of criminal matters was so extensive that Harry Hodge, the publisher of *Notable British Trials*, asked her to act as editor of the series. She went on to edit six in the series. Altogether Fryn's work extended to some nine novels, books of short stories, poems, plays, letters, a history of Burma and eight books on criminology.

With her direct style of writing and descriptive prose, Tennyson Jesse draws her readers in. Her best known book, *The Lacquer Lady*, is written from the point of view of a maid within the royal household in Burma, contrasting the horrors with the riches of the palace. *A Pin to see the Peepshow* concerns the unjust hanging of Edith Thompson.

As she aged, Tennyson Jesse's output slowed down and she died at her home in St John's Wood in 1958. She was remembered by her friends as being strikingly beautiful and her stentorian voice softened over the years.

Dame (Jocelyn) Barbara Hepworth   1903-1975
Sculptor and artist

Born in Wakefield, West Yorkshire, Barbara Hepworth was the eldest of four children. Her mother, Gertrude Allison (née Johnson), and especially her father, Herbert Raikes Hepworth, a civil engineer, encouraged her early interest in mathematics and art.

Educated at Wakefield Girls' High School and then Leeds School of Art for a year, Hepworth moved to the Royal College of Art in 1921 to study sculpture, where her contemporaries included Henry Moore and John Skeaping. Skeaping won the prestigious *Prix de Rome*: Hepworth was a runner up and was awarded a travelling scholarship, enabling her to study and travel in Italy, principally learning how to carve in stone. She married John Skeaping in Florence in 1925 and after their studies in Rome both returned to London in 1926, where they exhibited jointly. Their son Paul was born in 1929 – tragically he died in an air crash in 1953.

In the early 1930s Hepworth met the painter Ben Nicholson and lived with him in London. Their triplets were born in 1934 and they married in 1938, moving to Cornwall in 1939. They settled in St Ives, where Hepworth eventually acquired her own studio. In the early years of the war, with the demands of a young family and unable to carve, she ran a nursery school and concentrated on drawing. Her marriage to Ben Nicholson was dissolved in 1951.

During the 1950s Hepworth gained greater international recognition and her work increased in scale. Cancer was diagnosed in 1964, limiting her output, and her last years were spent in a wheelchair. She was created a Dame Commander of the British Empire in 1965 and received honorary degrees from a number of universities as well as from the Royal College of Art; she was a trustee of the Tate Gallery and Bard of the Cornish Gorseth, as *Gravyor* (sculptor). She died following an unexplained fire in her studio in 1975. Her Trewyn studio in St Ives was opened to the public in 1976 and is now part of the Tate Gallery, St Ives.

Hepworth spent the greater part of her working life in Cornwall where she was inspired by the light and natural forms around her.

Her work can be divided into distinct phases: the earlier stone carvings in Rome, progressing to simplified abstract forms in wood or stone when working with Ben Nicholson. During the early war years in Cornwall she concentrated on drawing and she returned to abstract and more figurative sculpture in the late 1940s. In her later years she experimented with bronze and other metals as well as multi-part sculptures.

Barbara Hepworth is regarded as one of the leading sculptors of the twentieth century and some of her more significant works include 'Wave' (1943), 'Pelagos' (1946), 'Contrapuntal forms' and 'Turning forms' for the Festival of Britain (1951). 'Single form' (1961-4), a large bronze memorial to the UN Secretary-General Dag Hammarskjöld, was positioned outside the United Nations buildings in New York.

Honour Hitchens 1771–1846
Fishwife

Honour Hitchens' claim to fame rests on the fact that she rescued her father from the clutches of the press gang. The story goes that while she was working beside a small stream, helping her father to clean fish, a member of the press gang seized her father and took him towards a naval ship.

Honour did not hear or see this, being slightly deaf. However, when she noticed her father's absence, she set off in pursuit and struck the man with a rough dogfish she was in process of cleaning. He relinquished his hold and Honour was able to pull her father away. This commotion was noticed by the women and boys in the neighbourhood, who came to help, praising and cheering Honour for her bravery.

Honour Hichens (sic) was baptised at Paul 12 May 1771, parents Stephen and Honour. She married Alexander Love in 1801 and died in Paul parish in 1846. The parish included Mousehole and part of Newlyn.

Emily Hobhouse 1860-1926
Humanitarian worker

Emily Hobhouse was responsible for raising public awareness about the plight of the women and children interned in camps by the British army during the Boer War in South Africa. She was revered in South Africa for her work, but branded as unpatriotic by the British press.

One of six children, Emily Hobhouse was born at St Ive. Her father,

Reginald Hobhouse, was the vicar and archdeacon of Bodmin. His family came from Somerset, whereas her mother Caroline (née Trelawny) was Cornish and descended from Bishop Jonathan Trelawny.

Emily Hobhouse was educated by her mother, then attended a finishing school in London for a short time in 1876. Returning to St Ive, she involved herself with parish work and after her mother's death in 1880 she cared for her father. Reading *The Times* to him, she became acquainted with world affairs and on his death in 1895 she received a substantial legacy.

Later the same year, she travelled to Minnesota to work in a remote pioneer mining settlement, where the promotion of temperance was her main concern. A broken engagement and an unwise investment in Mexico brought an end to her humanitarian efforts. She returned to London in 1898 and worked towards improving social conditions in deprived areas of London.

With the outbreak of the Boer War in South Africa in 1899, Hobhouse became concerned about the plight of the Boer women and children interned in concentration camps by the British army. To her sadness, her efforts to raise funds and public awareness were considered pro-Boer by some sectors of the British press.

As chairman of the South African Women and Children Distress Fund, she raised considerable funds and decided to visit the camps to distribute relief.

Obtaining permission to visit a military zone was fraught with problems and Lord Kitchener restricted her movements to Bloemfontein, with just one truck of supplies. Kitchener referred to her as 'That bloody woman', hence the title of John Hall's biography (Truran, 2008).

On arrival, Hobhouse found severe overcrowding, little water or sanitation, and food in short supply. She managed to effect some improvements but she decided to return to Britain to exert her influence on the Government.

Her findings embarrassed the authorities and in a Parliamentary debate it was stated that the priority was to support the British troops. To appease public opinion, the Government appointed an investigative committee headed by Lady Fawcett. Hobhouse's claims were largely substantiated, but the official report failed to disclose the full facts.

In 1901 Hobhouse decided to return to South Africa, with additional funds from her campaigns around the country. This time her entry was blocked and, after remaining a prisoner on board ship for five days, she was deported. Her next visit in 1903 was more successful, following the 1901 peace treaty. She involved herself in agricultural problems and taught lace-making, spinning and weaving to the Boer women. Back in London, she worked with the Women's Suffrage Movement and returned to South Africa to unveil the Women's Monument in Bloemfontein. On arrival she was too unwell to complete the journey and her speech was read in her absence.

Hobhouse lived in France and Italy, then in Cornwall at the beginning of WW1, although her charity work occasioned extensive European travel. She was chairman of the Fund to Aid Swiss Relief and worked to provide extra food for school children in Leipzig.

Having spent her savings on the relief of others, Hobhouse was overwhelmed to receive the generous sum of £2300 from the Boer women of South Africa in 1921, for the purchase of a house in St Ives. However, in 1923, in need of care and with increasing ill health, she moved to London, then Chichester and the Isle of Wight.

She died in a London nursing home, but her ashes were interred at the base of the Bloemfontein war memorial, a rare honour. Tributes poured in from South Africa after her death; to the Boer community she was the 'Angel of Love' and Mahatma Gandhi declared that she was one of the 'bravest and noblest of women'.

Mary Kelynack   1776-1855
Long distance walker

When Mary Kelynack made her epic walk from Cornwall to London, she captured the heart of the nation. Mary was born at Tolcarne, Madron, the daughter of Nicholas Tresize. In 1818, when she was aged 42, she married William Kelynack at Paul; they had no children. They lived at Newlyn and Mary helped her husband with his fishing boat and walked to Penzance to sell the fish.

1851 was the year of the Great Exhibition in London, orchestrated by Prince Albert, with Sir Henry Cole, an industrialist and designer, and Joseph Paxton, the gardener and designer. Some of the exhibits came by boat from Cornwall – an obelisk from Lamorna Quarry and objects made from serpentine. Mary Kelynack, now a widow, decided to visit the Great Exhibition herself. Not having the fare, she resolved to walk the 300 miles to London. This determined 75-year-old lady walked to London in five weeks. By the time that she arrived, she had achieved celebrity status.

After visiting the Exhibition, Mary had just 5 1/2 pence in her pocket, and was delighted to receive a gold sovereign from the Lord Mayor. She rode to the Mansion House in his coach for 'the best cup of tea' with the Mayoress. Queen Victoria recorded the event in her diary and sent her a sum of money. Gifts were also received from the pensioners at Greenwich, as well as a bible and a pound of snuff from other well wishers.

There was a report in the *Illustrated London News* referring to Mary 'Callinack', and Routledge published the story of her walk to London in *Aunt Mavor's Present For a Good Little Girl* (1856). While in London, Mary Kelynack enquired about the payment of her husband's naval pension, which had ceased on his death, but the outcome of this quest is not reported.

She returned by train in some triumph from Paddington to Exeter where she was met by the Mayor, and her fare from Exeter to Truro was paid by a Mr Prockter, a Launceston ironmonger. Mary died in Dock Lane, Penzance, and she was buried in St Mary's churchyard. There is a plaque to mark her cottage in Newlyn, and the Cornish sculptor Neville Burnard made a bust of her which was later displayed at the Royal Cornwall Polytechnic Society in Falmouth. As a footnote, the Australians have a Mary Callinack polka!

Dame Laura Knight (née Johnson)   1877-1970
Artist

The youngest of three sisters, Laura Knight was born in Long Eaton, Derbyshire. Her father, Charles Johnson, left home before Laura was born and the children were brought up in Nottingham by their mother Charlotte (née Bates), an art teacher.

Her mother sent Laura to be educated in France and then, when she was fourteen, to Nottingham School of Art. Here she met Harold Knight who was to become her husband. In 1895 Laura and her sister went with an aunt on a painting holiday to Staithes, near Whitby in Yorkshire. Harold Knight was asked to join them. Both Harold and Laura extended their stay, living on the sales of their pictures. They married in 1903.

Moving from Staithes in 1905, they made London their base, but spent some time living, studying and painting in Holland. Their next move, in 1907, was to a cottage and studio at the head of the Lamorna Valley near Newlyn, as they joined the second wave of Newlyn artists. They were to remain there until the end of WW2. Laura Knight was particularly attracted by her surroundings, the colours of the sea and the freshness of the countryside, splashing bright exuberant colours on to her canvases, aptly portraying the carefree spirit of the age – often causing a local stir by painting nude models outdoors. Some of her best paintings were done at this time.

In 1916 Laura Knight was commissioned by the Canadian Government to paint soldiers. During WW1 Harold Knight worked on the land as a conscientious objector, an unhappy time for them both, and they returned to London in 1918.

Always ready for a new challenge, Laura Knight painted dancers from Diaghilev's ballet company and when she accompanied her husband to Baltimore in 1926 she made sketches in the hospital wards set aside for Afro-Americans. A further change of direction came with an introduction to Bertram Mills and his circus, resulting in studies of circus artists. Boxing was another innovative theme she took up to some acclaim.

In 1929 she was made a DBE and in 1936 she was the first woman to be elected to full membership of the Royal Academy. In 1939, while the Knights were living in Colwall, near Malvern, Laura undertook to paint for the War Artists' Advisory Committee and in 1946 she received an assignment to record the war trials at Nuremberg.

After her husband's death in 1961, Laura Knight arranged exhibitions of their paintings and a retrospective of her work at the Royal Academy in 1965. She received many honours during her artistic career and was an honorary member of the Royal Society of Painters in Water Colours, the Royal Society of Painter-Etchers and Engravers, the Royal West of England Academy, the Society of Women Artists and the Royal Society of Portrait Painters. In addition, she received an honorary LLD from St Andrews University and an honorary D Litt from Nottingham University.

Many public London and provincial galleries have collections of her work, a truly impressive range in watercolours, oils and etchings.

Margaret Joyce Lidgey 1878-1951
Mine Manager

By taking over the running of the Magdalen Mine in 1914, Margaret Lidgey became the first female mine manager in the world.

Margaret Joyce Lidgey (also known as Marguerita or Rita) was born in Devoran near Truro. Her father Edwin became the manager of the Kennal Vale gunpowder factory, Ponsanooth, in 1887, and the family lived in the manager's house. Marguerita was fortunate enough to find employment as a clerk in the gunpowder factory office, where she learnt to type. She stayed in her job when the family moved to Lanner, not far from Redruth. Her father, however, changed his employment and became a commercial traveller, selling explosives to the mines in the area.

In 1913 two mining engineers opened up the disused Magdalen mine, Cosawes, named after an ancient pilgrimage chapel that had at one time stood close to the site. About four tons of black tin were pro-duced each month, using a magnetic separator. In 1914 the engineers left the mine and joined up to fight in WW1 and asked Marguerita to manage the mine in their absence. She went underground almost daily and perfected the art of vanning or ore dressing (washing the ore on a shovel), obtaining a high price for her tin, £450 for every ton. She did this work until one of the managers returned in 1918.

After the war, she presented a Cornish Cross for the lych gate at Lanner churchyard, to remember the men lost in WW1. During WW2, she worked as a Civil Defence Warden and secretary to the Prisoners of War committee. She was also involved in many local activities, such as the Women's Conservative Association and the rugby club. She enjoyed amateur dramatics, supported the local church and served on the Parish Council.

Marguerita stayed in Lanner until her death in Barncoose Hospital, Redruth in 1951.

Fanny Moody 1866-1945
Opera singer

One of 13 children, she was born Frances Moody, in Fore Street, Redruth, where her parents James Moody from Derbyshire and Eliza (née Datson, from Kea) had a photographic studio. Her father played the organ and all the children enjoyed music. Both Fanny and her sister Lily went on to become opera singers.

Fanny began her career by singing in chapel and school, earning her first concert fee when she was just twelve years old. In this way, she came to the notice of Mrs Gustavus Bassett from Tehidy, who recognised her talent and arranged for her to have singing lessons in London in 1882 with one of the leading contraltos, Charlotte Helen Stainton-Dalby. Attention was also paid to improving her social skills.

Most operas had always been performed in London but towards the end of the nineteenth century opera became popular in the provinces, in Manchester, Leeds, Newcastle and Birmingham.

In 1888, aged twenty-two, Fanny Moody had her first lead in an opera, singing Arline in *The Bohemian Girl* at the Court Theatre in Liverpool. When singing with the Carl Rosa Opera, a touring company, she met the bass Charles Manners (whose real name was Southcote Randal Mansergh) whom she married in 1890. They had made a successful tour of Cornwall the year before.

They both appeared in the London première of Tchaikovsky's *Eugene Onegin* in 1892, when Fanny Moody was the first English soprano to sing the role Tatiana.

In 1898 they formed the Moody-Manners Opera Company, performing at Covent Garden as well as in the provinces, North America and South Africa. At that time it was the largest opera company to tour Britain; it was disbanded before WW1.

Fanny Moody, sometimes known as Fanny Moody-Manners, became known as 'the Cornish Nightingale'; she had a wide repertoire, with some fifty roles from Wagner to Puccini. Her admirers showered her with gifts, a diamond bracelet from students in Edinburgh, and in South Africa the Cornish miners presented her with a diamond tiara inscribed with ONE AND ALL. When this was auctioned for charity in 1944, it fetched a mere £310.

Fanny Moody-Manners died in Dublin, surviving her husband by ten years.

Dorothy ('Dolly') Pentreath 1692–1777
Not quite the last speaker of Cornish

When Daines Barrington, lawyer and writer on a huge range of subjects from Anglo-Saxon literature to arctic exploration, came to Cornwall in 1768 looking for any traces of the Cornish language which had supposedly died out, he was introduced to Dolly Pentreath in Mousehole. She swore at him for several minutes 'in a language which sounded very like Welsh' and he became convinced she was the last speaker.

Later he found younger speakers, but Dolly may indeed have been the last who spoke it as her mother tongue, and she claimed she never spoke English till she was twenty.

She was a fish-seller, married to a Jeffery, but preferring to use her maiden name. In her old age she lived by a mixture of parish relief, fortune-telling and chattering away in Cornish to anyone who would pay her to do so. She died aged 85, claiming to be 102.

In 1850 Louis-Lucien Bonaparte (a scholarly nephew of Napoleon, who settled in England and became an expert on the minority languages of Europe, especially Basque) erected a granite memorial to her in the wall of Paul churchyard.

Agnes Prest 1503?-1557
Protestant martyr

Agnes Prest was burnt to death for her Protestant views. Her maiden name is unknown. She came from Northcot in the parish of Boyton and lived during the reigns of Henry VIII and Edward VI, times of massive religious change. When the Catholic Mary came to the throne in 1553, all the changes were put into reverse.

Although Agnes was illiterate, she had a good memory for the scriptures and was articulate in interpreting her views to others. For a while she worked as a domestic servant in Exeter and may well have witnessed the martyrdom of the Protestant Edward Benet. Returning to Cornwall, she married and took her husband's name, Prest. Problems arose when her husband tried to impose his strict Roman Catholic views, forcing her to attend mass, confession and processions. Agnes rebelled, abandoned her home and family and went about earning her living by spinning. Her husband brought her home, but she left again, unable to accept his religious discipline.

In 1555 Agnes Prest was arrested for heresy and taken to Launceston gaol. Three months elapsed before she was brought before Judge William Stanford, accused of denying the 'Real presence in the Sacrament'.

Found guilty, she was sent to Exeter, to appear before Bishop Turberville for sentence. He placed Prest in his own prison, warning her that the outcome could be burning. Here she earned certain privileges, working in the keeper's house, spinning and carding, and she could go into the city as she pleased. Her outspoken opinions and refusal to accept what she regarded as idolatry led to her re-imprisonment; she was brought again before Bishop Turberville and sentenced to death by burning.

The charge against her was 'Heresy chiefly against the Sacrament of the Altar and for speaking against idols'. Prest defended herself by reasoning that calling a piece of bread God, then worshipping it, was blasphemous and wrong. In accordance with the Apostles' Creed, Prest believed that the Body of Christ would remain in Heaven until the second coming.

Repentance, or even apparent repentance, would have earned her a reprieve, but she refused and she was burnt to death, aged 54, just outside Exeter city walls at Southernhay in August 1557. There is now a memorial to the Exeter martyrs in Denmark Road.

Doris Margaret (Dod) Procter (née Shaw)   1892-1972
Artist

Doris Procter's father, Frederick C Shaw, worked as a ship's doctor and her mother Eunice Mary (née Richards) was an artist, born on the Isle of Man and trained at the Slade School of Fine Art, London. Doris, their only daughter, was born in London but the family moved to Tavistock, Devon, when she was small. Dr Shaw died in 1907 and Doris, her brother and mother moved to Newlyn where both children were enrolled at the art school run by Stanhope and Elizabeth Forbes.

Ernest Procter was a fellow student and at his suggestion Doris went on to study at the Atelier Colarossi in Paris between 1910-11. Here she was greatly impressed by Cézanne and Renoir. Doris Shaw and Ernest Procter married in 1912 and their only child, Bill, was born in 1913.

In 1919-20 they worked in Rangoon, Burma, painting murals at the Kokine Palace. On their return, Doris Procter began painting portraits of young women, with crisp outlines, almost as though they were sculptures, and at this time she changed her name from Doris to Dod. The year 1927 gave Procter her greatest success when her painting 'Morning', with Cissie Barnes asleep on a bed, was voted the picture of the year at the Royal Academy Summer Exhibition. The picture, now in the Tate collection, was later bought for the nation by the *Daily Mail* and exhibited in regional art galleries and in New York. On her return to Newlyn, Procter was given a flag-waving reception, complete with a silver band.

During the 1930s, whilst continuing to paint women, her work became less stylised, with more colour and less definite outlines. Following the death of her husband in 1935, Procter travelled extensively, often with her friend, the painter Alethea Garstin. She was made a Royal Academician in 1942, a rare honour for a woman.

She died in Newlyn and was buried beside her husband at St Hilary, Marazion. Her work can be seen in many public collections throughout Britain as well as in Cornwall.

Lady Beatrice Frederika Wright
(other married name Rathbone)   1910-2003
Politician

When Beatrice Rathbone was elected as the Member of Parliament for Bodmin in 1941, she had the distinction of becoming only the second MP to have been born in the USA, as well as Cornwall's first woman Member of Parliament.

An only child, Beatrice was born in Connecticut to Frederika (née Hammond) and Frank Roland Clough. As a banker, his work involved overseas postings and the family generally accompanied him. Before she was ten years old, Beatrice had lived in Japan, Korea, China and Russia. She was educated at Radcliffe College, the women's college of Harvard University, then at Oxford University for two years. It was here that she met her future husband, John Rathbone, a student at Christ Church. They married in Boston, Massachusetts in 1932 and had two children, a son and a daughter.

In 1935, her husband was elected as the Conservative Member of Parliament for Bodmin, with Beatrice playing a key role in organizing his election campaign. At the outbreak of war in 1939, she was instrumental in organizing the evacuation of English children to America, sending her own children to stay with her uncle in Long Island, New York. In 1940 her life changed dramatically when her husband, a flying officer with the RAF Volunteer Reserve, was shot down during the Battle of Britain. Beatrice Rathbone stood as a candidate at the subsequent by-election and was returned unopposed as the MP for Bodmin.

As an active Member of Parliament, in 1941 she travelled to the USA to give a series of lectures, focusing on the part played by women in Britain during the war. Returning to the House of Commons, Beatrice Rathbone was a member of several committees, focusing her energies on infant welfare and women's issues. In some 70 speeches, she spoke about matters concerning her constituents in Bodmin, poor housing and the lack of piped water.

In May 1942 she married Paul Hervé Giraud Wright, a captain in the Kings Royal Rifle Corps, in Westminster Abbey. Their daughter Faith was born the following year, making Beatrice Wright the first serving member of parliament to give birth to a child. Despite living in Westminster, close to the House of Commons, there were practical problems in combining her role as a mother with her parliamentary responsibilities. With this in mind, in 1945 she decided not to seek re-election.

After the War, her husband joined the diplomatic service, with postings as ambassador in the Congo, Burundi and Lebanon, accompanied by his wife. He was knighted in 1975.

Lady Wright spent her later years in working to improve the position of the deaf. Her mother had lost her hearing following medication. In 1982, she co-founded Hearing Dogs for the Deaf (later called Hearing Dogs for Deaf People) and was the President until 1988. She was awarded an MBE in 1996 for her work with deaf people.

Together with her husband, Lady Wright converted to Catholicism in the 1980s. She died in March 2003 and her funeral mass was held at Westminster Cathedral.

Emily Stackhouse 1811-1870
Botanical artist

Emily Stackhouse's meticulous sketches and watercolours provided the illustrations for some of the most prestigious publications of her day.

Born in Modbury, Devon, she was the fifth of the six children of William Stackhouse and his wife Sarah (née Smith). Her father was the vicar at Modbury and he had sufficient resources to give his children a good education at home. In addition, he had connections with many of the landed families within Cornwall as well as friendships with some of the most respected botanists and naturalists of the time.

In 1830 William Stackhouse inherited Trehane, close to Probus in Cornwall, a Victorian mansion set in a 4000 acre estate. The family moved there in 1834, with Emily taking charge of the administration of the estate, writing in the farm ledgers in her careful hand, until 1861.

Widely travelled, she was a talented artist, painting from nature, observing the plants around her, writing both the English and Latin names of the Linnaean taxonomy on the reverse of each of her watercolours. Emily thought that classification was of utmost importance and, with this in mind, in 1846 she exhibited her work in the natural history category rather than artistic section in the fourteenth annual exhibition of the Royal Cornwall Polytechnic.

Her sketches received fulsome praise from the judges, together with a bronze medal, with similar results, and a second bronze medal, for a further entry in 1853.

Emily Stackhouse's work reached a wider audience when she was asked to provide the illustrations for several publications, notably books by the popular writer, Charles Alexander Johns. As well as *Forest Trees of Britain* and *A Week at the Lizard*, she provided hundreds of watercolours and sketches for him and was responsible for many of the illustrations in his well respected book *Flowers of the Field*, with her entries appearing anonymously. This particular book was reprinted many times and published by The Society for Promoting Christian Knowledge.

A scientific writer herself, Emily Stackhouse wrote a number of papers over the years, some unattributed, such as work on mosses and another article on rare plants in the Truro area. She is also said to have collected and classified nearly all the mosses in the country and left a legacy of over 600 watercolours.

When her father died in 1861, Emily and her sister Louisa moved to Truro. She died there in 1870 but was buried in the churchyard in Probus.

Mary Ann Tocker   1778-1853
Lawyer

Mary Ann Tocker is remembered for being the first woman in Cornwall to be charged with libel and the first woman to represent herself in court, sometimes called the first female lawyer.

Mary Ann Tocker was born in Tregony in 1778, the second of the six children of Dorothy Hearle and Thomas Wheare Tocker, from Gwinear. He worked as an attorney or lawyer but was in debt when he died, after a long illness, in 1796. One of Ann's brothers, Henry, followed in his father's footsteps, training to become a lawyer.

The libel case concerned Richard Gurney, son of the Rev Gurney of Tregony, who in 1813 was appointed by his father to the position of Vice Warden of the Stannaries. It was a post that brought considerable financial rewards. As part of the agreement, Henry Tocker was to be Richard Gurney's secretary and Richard Gurney himself was to lodge in the Tocker household in Plymouth, where the family were now living. Richard Gurney incurred many debts through gambling and he was out of the country between 1815 and 1819, unable to attend to his duties at the Stannary court. During his stay with the Tockers, Gurney paid no rent and Henry received no pay for his secretarial work. When Gurney's immediate family were approached for help, they implied that they had disowned him for his dissolute behaviour.

In 1817 a letter appeared anonymously in the *West Briton*, with the title 'An enemy to corruption'. The letter had been written jointly by Henry and Mary Ann Tocker. Henry later distanced his involvement, to prevent Richard Gurney from jeopardising his career as a lawyer in Plymouth. As Vice Warden, Richard Gurney had the power to do this. Mary Ann refused to back down and was then charged with libel, to appear in court in Bodmin.

On 4 August 1818, Mary Ann, Henry and another sister entered a crowded courtroom. The judge presumed that no-one would be defending the case and expressed surprise when Henry replied to say that the case would be defended by his sister. The charge was read out, 'Committing a most serious offence, in slandering the character of a gentleman in high judicious situation, by imputing to him practices of the greatest criminality, in a letter published in a newspaper called the *West Briton)*. The letter claimed that Richard Gurney had neglected his duties as a judge while being outlawed for debt, that he had demanded money from suitors before he would allow them to appear in the Stannary court and that he had also obtained his position through the 'borough-mongering system'. The prosecution only asked the editor to confirm that Mary Ann had written the letter, no further witnesses were called.

Mary Ann then spent two hours defending her case, amidst frequent interruptions by the judge. She quoted from several legal texts, making the point that she had not written out of malice but to expose injustices and she could prove her accusations in written evidence. However, the judge ruled that Mary Ann could not produce any letters or call witnesses. Summing up the case he urged the jury to return a verdict of guilty, claiming that Mary Ann had written a libellous letter. Retiring to consider the case, the jury asked to view the letters that Mary Ann had wanted to read out in court. They took just 30 minutes to return a verdict of not guilty, amidst loud cheering from the crowds.

Trewman's Exeter Flying Post was the first newspaper to give a report of the trial on 13 August, followed by *The Times* on 17 August. Other writers wrote their accounts, including William Cobbett, who wrote a summary from America, and Mary Ann published her own version. Her finances improved considerably when she received donations from both The Devon County Club and the *Morning Chronicle*.

Little is known about Mary Ann's life after the trial. She was living in Plymouth in 1841, with her brother Henry, now a successful lawyer, and she died in Penryn in 1853, close to the rest of her family in Falmouth.

In 1843, the Libel Act changed the law to allow a defendant to say that what had been said was true and in the public interest. The Act confirmed the position taken by Mary Ann at the court in Bodmin in 1818.

Elizabeth Treffry 15th century
Defender of Fowey

When the French attacked Fowey in 1457, Elizabeth Treffry, in her husband Thomas Treffry's absence, defended Place House against them, reputedly pouring molten lead from the roof onto the attackers.

Lady Clara Coltman Vyvyan (née Rogers) 1886-1976
Traveller and writer

Lady Clara Coltman Vyvyan was born in Queensland, Australia, the second daughter of Edward Powys Rogers, of Torilla Plains, Queensland, and his wife Charlotte (née Williams) from Tregye, near Truro; there were also two sons from the marriage. The family moved to Cornwall when she was two years old, residing at Burncoose, Gwennap.

Lady Vyvyan took a degree in Social Science at the London School of Economics.

During WW1 she based herself at the Women's University Settlement in Southwark and worked amongst the London poor. She was an indefatigable war worker, helping serve meals to the troops in Rouen and looking after Belgian internees at a Dutch camp.

After her marriage in 1929 to Colonel Sir Courtenay Bourchier Vyvyan of Trelowarren the pattern of her life changed. She devoted her energies to organising the estate garden at Trelowarren and became involved in local concerns and work with the WVS (later the RWVS), performing the duties expected in her position as Lady Vyvyan. As the titles of her books indicate, she was a practical gardener, happiest when wearing her informal gardening outfit. She sold produce to local hotels. *Amateur Gardening for Pleasure and Profit* was published in 1951 and *Letters from a Cornish Garden* in 1972. She also wrote about her great love for the area in such books as *Helford River* (1956) and *A Cornish Year* (1958).

Lady Vyvyan was a keen traveller as well as a prolific writer. *Down the Rhone on Foot* (1955) was a description of a four hundred mile trek from the river's glacier source to the Mediterranean delta, undertaken at the age of 67. Her friends Daphne du Maurier and Foy Quiller-Couch accompanied her for part of this journey.

Temples and Flowers, a Journey to Greece appeared in 1955 and *Arctic Adventure* in 1961, an account of travelling 600 miles by canoe in 1926 with Gwen Dorrien Smith and native American guides along Canada's Rat River to Fort Yukon in Alaska.

During WW2 Trelowarren was occupied by the army. When her husband died in 1941, Lady Vyvyan moved into the smaller wing of the house. Her cousin, John, took over the main house in 1950. Lady Vyvyan died at Trelowarren and her ashes were scattered in the gardens.

Annie Willliams   1860-1943
Teacher and suffragette

Annie Williams abandoned her teaching career in 1908, in order to devote herself full time to promoting and taking part in the suffragette movement.

She was born in Feock, close to Truro, where her father James Cargoe Williams, worked as a carpenter. Her mother was Catherine Marshall and there were two other daughters and a son. After primary school, Annie moved to Truro, living in lodgings while attending the Truro Diocesan Training College as a Queen's Scholar. Her first position as a schoolmistress, was at Cubert, on the North Coast, moving on to be headmistress at Crantock Public Elementary School, Newquay.

In 1907 Annie Williams joined the Women's Social and Political Union (WSPU), a women-only political movement campaigning for women's suffrage. The following year, she spent her summer holiday working for the WSPU in Bristol and it was here that she met her future partner, Lettice Floyd. She returned to teaching, but in November 1908 she attended a WSPU meeting in Plymouth and decided to become a full time organiser for the movement. Her sister, Edith, who lived at Devoran, later took over the Cornwall Branch.

Annie Williams continued with her support for the WSPU, working in Newcastle-upon-Tyne to support the election there and opening a WSPU shop. She moved on to act as organizer for Huddersfield and Halifax, then for the whole of Wales. Here she organized campaigns in various sea-side resorts and had time to go off hill walking.

In 1912 Annie Williams took part in a window smashing protest outside the House of Commons, together some 200 other activists. She was sentenced to spend a month in Holloway prison. Here Annie Williams and Lettice Floyd took part in a hunger strike and were forcibly fed. Both suffragettes were later awarded the WSPU Hunger Strike Medal for their courageous behaviour. In that same year, she was attacked by the crowd after speaking for the WSPU at a rally in Canford, Dorset.

At the start of WW1 the suffragettes called off their campaign and together Annie Williams and Lettice Floyd moved to Berkswell, near Coventry, living quite openly in a same sex relationship. Here they helped to establish the Women's Institute in Berkswell and Annie was the President for a number of years.

When Lettice Floyd died in 1934, she left Annie Williams a sum of £3000 and an annual income of £300. Moving back to Cornwall in her later years, Annie died in Truro in 1943.

In 1928 the Representation of the People Act gave all women over 21 the right to vote.